My Journey Discovering The True Gospel.

2° EDITION √ Revised √ Corrected √ Improved √ Expanded √ Renewed

Domingo González Jr.

(Alias Martín García)

MY JOURNEY DISCOVERING THE TRUE GOSPEL - 2ND EDITION - DOMINGO GONZÁLEZ JR.

First edition. November 4, 2023.

Copyright © 2023 Domingo Gonzalez.

ISBN: 979-8223087441

Written by Domingo Gonzalez.

Also by Domingo Gonzalez

Una Gloria Diferente
A Different Kind of Glory
Un Tipo de Gloria Diferente - Domingo Gonzalez Jr.
Mi Travesía Descubriendo el Evangelio Verdadero - 2da Edición
Esqueletos no Armário - Memórias do Filho de um Pastor.- 2º. Edição.
Domingo González Jr.
Minha Jornada Descobrindo o Verdadeiro Evangelho.
My Journey Discovering The True Gospel - 2nd Edition - Domingo
González Jr.
Um Tipo Diferente de Glória - Domingo González Jr.

My Journey Discovering The True Gospel. 2nd. Edition.

Domingo González Jr.

(Alias Martín García)

2023

Cover designed with images generated on: https://firefly.adobe.com/

THANKS

I want to thank God with all my heart for all those people who never gave up and have never given up, those who are with the Lord and those who are still living, those who remained and who have remained in the truth and not only They have maintained it, but they have defended it and spread it despite the insults and attacks of false Christians and the world.

People like Paul Washer, David Wilkerson, Juan Manuel Vaz, Will Graham, Leonard Ravenhill, Haziel Rodríguez, Steven Lawson, John MacArthur, Sugel Michelen, Miguel Núñez, Vodie Bauchman, John Huss, John Piper, Martin Luther, William Tynsdale, Charles Finney , Charles Spurgeon, Jonathan Edwards, John Wesley, R.C. Sproul, A.W. Tozer... and it would take a thousand pages to mention them all, but I thank God and them who never gave up and have never given up to bring us the truth of the gospel in the midst of so many false teachers, false pastors and false prophets.

DEDICATION

I dedicate this book to all Christians who do not want to live a mediocre Christian life, but rather seek the truth and desire to live a life that pleases God.

And if you bought this book or it was given to you as a gift, it is because you are one of them; So, This Book Is Dedicated to You!

CONTENT

THANKS

    DEDICATION

    INTRODUCTION

    CHAPTER 1: Beginning of the Journey.

    CHAPTER 2: Discovering the Biblical Truth about Blessing – Being Blessed.

    CHAPTER 3: Discovering the Biblical Truth about Healing.

    CHAPTER 4: Discovering the Biblical Truth about Prayer.

    CHAPTER 5: Discovering the Biblical Truth about Faith.

    CHAPTER 6: Discovering the Biblical Truth about the Invariability of God.

    CHAPTER 7: Discovering The Biblical Truth about The Message.

    CHAPTER 8: Discovering the Biblical Truth about Cost.

    CHAPTER 9: Discovering the Biblical Truth about Identity.

    CHAPTER 10: Discovering the Biblical Truth about Music in the Church.

    ANNEXES

    Exhibit 1: What's wrong with the "prosperity gospel"?

    Exhibit 2: A Much More Subtle Prosperity Gospel

    Annex 3: Why Am I Against the Prosperity Gospel?

    FINAL WORDS

    RECOMMENDED BIBLIOGRAPHY

INTRODUCTION

Hello my precious men and women, I am Domingo González, the teacher Bubba, "Alias Martín García"

Many years ago, Leonard Ravenhill stated that in recent times it would be chaos because everyone would claim to have the truth, that time has already arrived and we can see hundreds of pastors claiming to have the true gospel. If you are one of the people who is really interested in knowing the true gospel, with this short book I hope to help you in the midst of this chaos.

I like simplicity when speaking without going to the extreme, and in this book I hope to express myself in the same way. My idea is that my books can be read by a 5-year-old child to a 90-year-old old man without problems, and I personally consider that all Christian books should be like this, easy to read and understand. I hope to achieve this goal.

Well, let's start with the presentation of the book.

Since I was a child, I have been in the Christian church, from Pentecostal to free, including some that I don't even know what category they fall into. One was so, but so free that the pastor had a son with the prophet of the church, who by the way was not his wife.

In my life I have known a thousand ways of teaching and living the gospel, some super liberal, others very rigid. The interesting thing is that they all say they have the true gospel. Some are so convincing and speak with such great apparent sincerity that one says: "it has to be as he says." Others give you Bible verses more crooked than a pig's tail, but since they give Bible verses one says "if he gives biblical verses have to be right"

Others use the most effective technique so far and that is to get us so excited that we don't even care to check in the Bible if the verses they give, in their correct context, agree with what they want to teach. They know that we live in an era where emotions rule and if they are skilled at manipulating people's emotions, they can make them believe whatever they want. (For this reason, I consider that a book that I have in mind and I pray God gives me the blessing to write and which I plan to title "Christianity in the midst of an Emotionalist Society" would be a good consideration to read.)

At one point in my life, I was ambushed by all these teachings about the gospel and I felt all those voices in my head each one affirming that they were right and I had to go to the source, that is, The Bible.

In this short book I will explain my journey discovering the gospel after more than 35 years of hearing about the gospel and seeing it lived in a thousand ways. (it's really more than 35 years, but I don't want people to think I'm too old, so let's leave it at 35)

Through this book I do not intend to impose my discovery, but rather to encourage each person to carry out their own search.

Come on, get on the Bubba Bus and join me on this journey.

CHAPTER 1
Beginning of the Journey.

Being in the city where I live, things became strong in my head regarding this topic of the gospel, because I began to see how a pastor who has a somewhat peculiar way of living the gospel, who had run as a presidential candidate and for the At the end of his electoral campaign he presented a very, very impious music group, then the celebration of his daughter's 15th birthday was a crazy celebration.

Also on the local radio I heard a pastor talk about "The Gospel of the Kingdom" and when he explained his gospel I realized that it was nothing more than that gospel that progressive Christians live where it is emphasized that God is there to fulfill our dreams, make us rich. , healthy and happy.

On the other hand, he had some neighbors from a church who assured his disciples in his house of peace that if they converted everything would be peace and harmony in his home.

Apart from that, in my backpack I had the gospel that I had been taught in all the churches where we had been. (Read my book "Skeletons in the Closet" to understand better)

In my backpack I had what they taught me that you couldn't say you were sick because you were accepting the illness and you didn't have faith. Even if you were dying of pain, if they asked you how you were, you had to say "Healed by the wounds of Christ" and nor could it occur to you to say that you were wrong if you were wrong.

In my backpack was the one who had to confess the opposite because words have power. That is, if you were sad you had to say that you were happy, if you felt bad you had to say that you felt good. I no longer knew if he was being a liar or if he was really confessing the opposite.

There were many occasions when I said that I was in pain and the other brothers scolded me because I was accepting the illness.

With that alone the backpack was very heavy, eventually I realized that the weight was too much and that I was not free, I could not be sincere, I had to say what others expected me to say because otherwise they would call me a lack of faith or lack of spirituality. I felt hypocritical, but if that was the gospel, if that was how the Christian life was to be lived, well, I had to do it that way.

In that backpack was the gospel Happy, Happy, where we are assured that God is there to fulfill our dreams and to make us happy and if he takes something from us it is to give us something better, that Jesus became poor to make us rich, which is why poverty is a curse and that a sign that God is with someone is that they are doing well financially.

I think that made the backpack almost knock me to the ground because all my life I struggled to make money and I hadn't been able to achieve it. To make matters worse, there were the other Christian brothers who had the same teachings and if they saw you without money, they could not accept that God was with you because you were not prosperous, which is why they did not accept any advice or anything from you.

In my backpack were memories of times when they denigrated me by comparing me to other people and told me "X already has a house and a car and you have nothing."

Around that time, I found a video on YouTube of a certain Paul Washer who seemed to me to preach in such a timeless, firm way, as if he gave too much seriousness to the gospel and had a somewhat different gospel compared to modern pastors, then they began to Videos of a certain David Wilkerson appeared to me and the video of "cries of Anguish" took me out of place.

On the other hand, I heard a pastor named Nahum talk about people he had never heard of before, according to him courageous Christians, with unwavering faith, who lived an exemplary Christian life. He mentioned a certain Whitefield, Finney, Edwards, Wesley, Spurgeon, Ravenhill among others.

The modern church presented me with a God so idiotic that you could force him to do things by reminding him of what he had said because "He cannot refuse to do what his word says" or he could be manipulated by declaring and decreeing. They presented me with a Jesus so loving that I could very easily call him stupid and idiotic, one of pure love, who accepts everything, does not correct, does not demand, does not condemn.

All of this made me feel like my head was pounding, it hurt horribly and I desperately asked myself WHAT IS THE TRUE GOSPEL? WHAT IS GOD LIKE? WHAT IS JESUS LIKE?

I had no choice but to make a decision. I told myself, I am going to read the New Testament as many times as necessary until I manage to discover what the true gospel is and what Jesus is really like. Apart from that, I decided to investigate all those people that Pastor Nahum said in that morning prayer session.

I remember that it was a time when I did not have internet (strangely) and I would ask a favor from a relative of the people here to download the books for me and I would write down the names of each man of God that they recommended in the books and I would ask that boy to do me the favor of downloading it. To the glory of God he never complained.

Since he had no job, no television or internet, he distributed his time to reading the New Testament.

The rest of the time I read about all those men of God and some books by Paul Washer; all with bibles in hand. I knew that if I read the books, checking everything in the Bible, it would take me longer to read the books, but I wanted to know the truth and nothing but the truth.

In the process there were days when I had to stop reading and I would go out to the patio with my hands on my head, frustrated and with a headache, because in my life I had heard a thousand sermons and what I was learning from the New Testament went against many things that I was convinced of as to what the gospel was, who Jesus was and what HE was like.

Although my mother instilled in me the study of the scriptures since I was a child, she had never dedicated me to a serious study of the scriptures. But this time was different because at this time there was an immense desperation to know the truth once and for all.

In the midst of all this I realized that I had a problem that many have today. I was having a hard time accepting the truths that the Bible itself was teaching me, even when I saw that those truths, I was learning were not crazy things, but the gospel that the apostles and men of God of ancient times like Finney had already lived., Edwards, Whitefield, Spurgeon, the beloved Puritans.

I realized that my problem was that I did not want to give up all those teachings that I had treasured for years and which made me feel proud and gave me a feeling of confidence and security. It was horrible for me to feel, so ignorant! Today I understand that the apostle Paul also had to give up everything he thought he knew and called all that GARBAGE (Philippians 3: 4-8)

For many people that is still his treasure. Their spiritual lives are like stagnant waters and some have to sell themselves to the progressive gospel to feel something new when what they have to do is go back, to the old path, to the true gospel that those beautiful men of God practiced.

On one occasion I went out to the patio crying, I hid so that no one would see me and I told God: "I can't resist anymore, I renounce everything I thought I knew about you, about Jesus and the gospel, and I decide to receive everything that I want to teach, I no longer resist what your word says."

At that moment I felt like the most ignorant person in the world, I felt like a recent convert who knows nothing about the Bible, at that moment I emptied myself, at that moment I threw aside everything I had learned for the year and which was a treasure. for me and what I was proud of and made me feel with "Status" for all the years in the gospel and for all the word I had heard for years (usually teachings with separate verses taken out of their context)

From that moment on, every word, every sermon, every teaching I ever heard must go through the exhaustive filter of the scriptures before it can be considered true. The truth is a super strange sensation.

One of the quotes that changed my life was: Hebrews 11:36-39 I couldn't understand why, having spent my entire life in the gospel, I had never heard sermons on that quote, the sermons were always up to verse 35, everything was cool. But when reading Hebrews 11: 36-39 I understood that the true gospel was not as beautiful or as happy as the prosperity gospel and Barak show in his song.

I wanted to talk to my parents, I wanted to talk to several other people, but they all have the resistance that I had to the scriptures and they ended up treating me like a crazy person.

And I just said to myself, how can I be crazy if everything is in the Bible in its correct context? How crazy if it is the gospel that men of God who changed history lived until their death?

I remember that one time God made me tell my parents that it was necessary to go back, the verse that God asked me to tell them was "Thus says the Lord: Stand in the ways, and look, and ask for the ancient paths, what is the good path, and walk in it, and you will find rest for your soul. But they said, "We will not walk" (Jeremiah 6:16).

And just as it says at the end of the verse, "we will not walk" like that they did. And the truth is I understand how difficult it is. It implies renunciation, it implies killing pride and it implies humility and the truth, no matter how humble they appear, most Pastors do not have it. And giving up what for them is a treasure is difficult because as Spurgeon said "What for the Apostle Paul was garbage, many pastors have as a curriculum."

I remember once being all excited writing to my parents, URLs to YouTube videos of Paul Washer, David Wilkerson, Paolo Junior, and preaching websites of Spurgeon and A.W. Tozer about prayer, FROM A GALLITO CELL PHONE as we call it here. They are those old cell phones that you had to press a key several times to write a letter. I didn't have a phone and they lent me that one, and with that I wanted to share what for me were treasures. Just imagine writing more than 50 URLs like: http/xww.ccel.org/ccel/wesley/journalhtml

LETTER BY LETTER! FROM A "GALLITO" CELL PHONE! Press a hard key three or 4 times to write A LETTER!!! A fucking letter! I was all excited to share the revolution and spiritual awakening that was happening within me as I returned to the old path and the response was a piece of ice and telling me that reading drives people crazy. They didn't watch a single video; they didn't read a single teaching from Spurgeon... They broke my heart; the truth is I did it with so much love!

But who would think of wanting to teach something to people who have been in the ministry for more than twenty years and who were the ones who taught me to pray? Who would think? It occurred to someone who believed they were humble enough to learn from people who did a thousand times more for the kingdom of God in one year than they have done in a lifetime in ministry. And the truth is that is where I learned about humility in the pastorate. A man of God once said that it was incongruous to call yourself a Christian and have a reluctance to learn.

But Sunday, get to the point, what did you learn? I already think that several things were understood, but I could summarize what I learned this way:

CHAPTER II
Discovering The Biblical Truth about Blessing/Being Blessed.

For years I have heard that God's will is for us to be enriched. Among many others, they use the biblical quote from 2 Corinthians 8: 9 "For you know the grace of our Lord Jesus Christ, that for your sakes he became poor while he was rich, so that through his poverty you might become rich."

They say that Abraham was rich and that all the patriarchs were rich. They teach that if someone is not blessed, that is, does not have money, you should not listen to anything they say.

I remember a leader telling me that for her this was a horrible burden, because sometimes she didn't have money, but she went into debt to have things, so that the brothers in the church would see her "Blessed" and could pay attention to her when it was her turn to give a message. word or advice. She told me that she said she felt horrible pressure to have a car and a house and always wear new clothes, and when she didn't have money, she began to doubt her spirituality and began to examine herself to see what sin she was in, that she wasn't "blessed."

This is another of the traps of the progressive gospel or prosperity gospel that says that God is there to bless us, give us money and fulfill our dreams. It is taught that if God takes something from you it is to give you something better. Nothing could be further from the truth.

God is not here to fulfill our dreams; we are here to fulfill his dreams. If God does not take something away, it is not to give us something better, but to show us that he commands.

Today it is a law in almost all Christian denominations that if you see someone with money it is because God is with that person. And they are the first on the list to run for any leadership.

I remember someone once told me "Until you have as much money as Pastor "a tremendous man of God"

It is quite obvious to understand that it is not bad to be rich or want to have good things, but we must be clear that the true gospel is not about having wealth nor that a person's spirituality is measured by how much wealth they have because we would have to assume that many current antichrists "they are people of God"

1 Cor 4:11: Even unto this present hour we both hunger, and thirst, and are naked, and are buffeted, and have no certain dwelling place;

Luc 9:23-25: And he said to them all, If any man will come after me, let him deny himself, and take up his cross daily, and follow me. For whosoever will save his life shall lose it: but whosoever will lose his life for my sake, the same shall save it. For what is a man advantaged, if he gain the whole world, and lose himself, or be cast away?

Mat 6:19-20: Lay not up for yourselves treasures upon earth, where moth and rust doth corrupt, and where thieves break through and steal: But lay up for yourselves treasures in heaven, where neither moth nor rust doth corrupt, and where thieves do not break through nor steal:

Heb 11:37-38: They were stoned, they were sawn asunder, were tempted, were slain with the sword: they wandered about in sheepskins and goatskins; being destitute, afflicted, tormented; (Of whom the world was not worthy:) they wandered in deserts, and in mountains, and in dens and caves of the earth.

1 Tim 6:8-9: And having food and raiment let us be therewith content. But they that will be rich fall into temptation and a snare, and into many foolish and hurtful lusts, which drown men in destruction and perdition.

CHAPTER III
Discovering The Biblical Truth about Healing.

I experienced this topic about healing closely all my life with my mother, who used to be a very sickly person.

In my life I always heard sermons saying that if you were sick, it was because you were in sin, since for the children of God illness is illegal and if you were sick, it was because you opened doors to the devil through a sin because illness is from the devil. I heard sermons from pastors like Yiye Ávila where they affirmed a lot of things that left one cold. They make you feel really bad for being sick and make you understand why so many people like that are dying, if you ask them how they are they answer "Blessed and Prospered", "In Victory"

I remember that my father also preached the same thing and it was super interesting because as I said, my mother used to be a woman who got sick frequently, so when my mother got sick due to my father's preaching, comments began in the church that if my mother was sick was surely because she was in sin or was a woman with a lot of lack of faith, which by the way is another of the things that are said, if you are sick it is because you are in sin or you have a lack of faith.

At home everything was very funny because my dad always preached that and since he almost never got sick there were no problems. But guess what? Yes, the same thing you should be thinking, suddenly my father began to get sick continuously and miraculously the sermons saying that if you were sick, it was due to lack of faith or because you were in sin, stopped.

And the biblical truth is that God has no obligation to heal you. Many people close to God are likely to die sick. That does not mean that we should resign ourselves to the disease. But the fact that we are sick does not mean that we are in sin, that God is not with us or that we lack faith as many teach.

No one can deny that Timothy was a man of God, however, as the Apostle Paul states, Timothy was continually sick: 1 Timothy 5:23: "Don't drink water anymore, but use a little wine because of your stomach and your FREQUENT DISEASES"

CHAPTER IV
Discovering The Biblical Truth about Prayer.

It is obvious that being in church since childhood one has heard many sermons about prayer, and being trained by my mother from a very young age in this art that is nothing more than the "natural" expression of the being to communicate with its creator, it is Obviously, according to me, I already knew how to pray, but when I arrived in the city where I am and things began to happen to me (which you will have to read my book "Skeletons in the Closet: Memoirs of a Pastor's Son" so that you know which ones, because I am not going to tell them here why I would do this book longer than I intend it to be) I found myself having to do a lot of research on prayer.

I remember that I started by searching the Bible for all the prayers that appear in the Bible because I needed to find prayers that produced God's answer. I was at a time when we were going hungry and I had been taught that Christians did not suffer unless they were in sin or outside the will of God, so I had a lot of doubts in my head and I examined myself a lot and if it was not sinning the problem, maybe the problem was that I wasn't praying well, so I started doing all this research.

As I asked God to teach me how to pray from scratch, I began to analyze my own way of praying. There were days when I didn't know how to present myself before God because if we continued to be hungry it was surely because God was not listening to my prayers and if He was not listening to my prayers, it was surely because I was praying wrong. As I already explained, I had never been taught that God could allow one to suffer.

I read a lot about how Charles Spurgeon, one of the prayer heroes of ancient times, prayed, I read many teachings on prayer from him and many other men of prayer, I read many books, I analyzed every prayer in the Bible, I delighted in studying the last prayer of Jesus on earth (John 17) And surprisingly the situation did not change no matter how much I acquired knowledge about prayer, but I did change.

I began to realize that the teachings of Declare, decree, the "I prophesy", Remind God of his word... are a rubbish of teachings. We are taught that if you remind God of the scriptures, you practically put him on the ropes and because he should solve you.

I was never taught about the sovereignty of God; I was never taught that when he pleases if he pleases, he will do something. HE is not our errand boy nor can we put him on the ropes by reminding him of his promises. He is sovereign, and although it is good and necessary to learn to pray in the right way, even praying in the right way, if he does not want to do something he will not do it and he does not have to give us reasons why he does not do it.

I remember a Christian neighbor who used to pray very loudly so much that I heard her clearly and she prayed for an hour or more and normally of that hour of prayer she spent 45 minutes declaring, decreeing and prophesying and the rest of the time she prayed for sins. of others.

I remember saying to myself, "There's something that doesn't fit me, this girl doesn't beg, she doesn't beg, she doesn't ask, she just declares and decrees, she doesn't ask for forgiveness for her own sins, she doesn't ask that God change her, but it's the others." that should be changed" and at that moment I said to myself "Dominguito, you have to read a lot of the Bible because you have to see if what this girl is doing is correct."

As always, I maintained my principle that if something was not taught or practiced by Jesus or the apostles, I could not accept it as truth. So, I began to investigate what the Bible taught about prayer, what Jesus and the apostles taught and practiced and I dedicated myself to analyzing the structures and content of the prayers that appear in the Bible that were answered and a change began within from me.

I began to realize how lying and unbiblical this teaching about declaring, decreeing and prophesying is, because that type of teaching was never taught or practiced by Jesus or by the apostles or by anyone in the Bible, but it was something that began in the mid-19th century.

I understood that the most correct prayer is the one that is made in humiliation, with sincerity, with prayer, understanding that, although the Bible says that we can confidently enter before the throne of his grace, well, we are children, he is still God and deserves fear. , reverence (Malachi 1:6)

I was moved and I still love Jesus' last prayer for the apostles. I believe that, if there were no other example of prayer in the Bible, with that prayer made by Jesus we can learn everything we need to know about prayer. How much confidence! How much simplicity! How much reverence! How much sincerity! How much love!

Today there is so much mechanical prayer, so much prayer without soul, so much prayer without sincerity, we pray as in theory we should pray so that those who hear approve my way of praying, but they remain owed in terms of sincerity. Many are hypocritical, learned prayers, where the heart is not opened to God, but rather what should be said is said. And that's it!

I am one of those who thinks that just by watching someone pray you can know everything there is to know about a person. Some change their voice, others want to appear broken and even fake cry, others pray the way they are supposed to, they should pray, but a prayer with such simplicity, sincerity, love, trust and reverence towards our "Abba" as that of John 17 we will almost never find it.

I remember one time I was going to pray with some brothers and I started praying the way I knew I was supposed to pray and I had to stop praying because I realized I wasn't being sincere, I wasn't being real, so I started again. new and although perhaps the prayer was not what people expected, it was real and sincere and unfortunately people have become accustomed to hypocrisy and they always expect all the decoration that a prayer should have and when they hear a prayer without decorations and without change of voice the sentence no longer seems very correct to them.

In summary, I discovered that all the prayers that I found in the Bible that were accepted before God had the same characteristics: Humiliation, Sincerity, Truth, Spirituality, Simplicity, Confidence, Fear,

Freedom, Authority, Without hypocrisy, Without arrogance and obviously in none I found no one declaring, prophesying and decreeing or wanting to force God to do something by reminding him of what he said, yes, on several occasions he was reminded of what he once promised, but it was never done with the intention of forcing him to act in any way. as is intended to be done today.

Like I said, these for me, discoveries about prayer that maybe you already knew didn't change the situation, but they changed me. I hope to God to be able to publish a book that I have in mind, which I want to title "What I learned about prayer in my most difficult moment" where I will explain in more detail everything I learned.

John 17

These words spake Jesus, and lifted up his eyes to heaven, and said, Father, the hour is come; glorify thy Son, that thy Son also may glorify thee:

As thou hast given him power over all flesh, that he should give eternal life to as many as thou hast given him.

And this is life eternal, that they might know thee the only true God, and Jesus Christ, whom thou hast sent.

I have glorified thee on the earth: I have finished the work which thou gavest me to do.

And now, O Father, glorify thou me with thine own self with the glory which I had with thee before the world was.

I have manifested thy name unto the men which thou gavest me out of the world: thine they were, and thou gavest them me; and they have kept thy word.

Now they have known that all things whatsoever thou hast given me are of thee.

For I have given unto them the words which thou gavest me; and they have received them, and have known surely that I came out from thee, and they have believed that thou didst send me.

I pray for them: I pray not for the world, but for them which thou hast given me; for they are thine.

And all mine are thine, and thine are mine; and I am glorified in them.

And now I am no more in the world, but these are in the world, and I come to thee. Holy Father, keep through thine own name those whom thou hast given me, that they may be one, as we are.

While I was with them in the world, I kept them in thy name: those that thou gavest me I have kept, and none of them is lost, but the son of perdition; that the scripture might be fulfilled.

And now come I to thee; and these things I speak in the world, that they might have my joy fulfilled in themselves.

I have given them thy word; and the world hath hated them, because they are not of the world, even as I am not of the world.

I pray not that thou shouldest take them out of the world, but that thou shouldest keep them from the evil.

They are not of the world, even as I am not of the world.

Sanctify them through thy truth: thy word is truth.

As thou hast sent me into the world, even so have I also sent them into the world.

And for their sakes I sanctify myself, that they also might be sanctified through the truth.

Neither pray I for these alone, but for them also which shall believe on me through their word;

That they all may be one; as thou, Father, art in me, and I in thee, that they also may be one in us: that the world may believe that thou hast sent me.

And the glory which thou gavest me I have given them; that they may be one, even as we are one:

I in them, and thou in me, that they may be made perfect in one; and that the world may know that thou hast sent me, and hast loved them, as thou hast loved me.

Father, I will that they also, whom thou hast given me, be with me where I am; that they may behold my glory, which thou hast given me: for thou lovedst me before the foundation of the world.

O righteous Father, the world hath not known thee: but I have known thee, and these have known that thou hast sent me.

And I have declared unto them thy name, and will declare it: that the love wherewith hou hast loved me may be in them, and I in them.

CHAPTER V
Discovering the Biblical Truth about Faith.

Who knew that Hebrews 11 could be so twisted? But the truth is that one cannot ask that question in the midst of such tremendous progressive Christianity, where they will always be able to distort biblical quotes no matter how difficult it may seem.

I think faith has always been something complicated to explain and understand. Although there are apparently clear passages, this generation of Christians has practically become experts in twisting biblical verses and people have been taught a type of faith that the apostles never practiced, a type of faith that does not appear in the Bible. of faith that is closer to positivism and humanism than to the Bible, a faith that, as Itiel Arroyo says, is probably a Christian version of superstition.

An unbiblical faith of confession and suppression, there are things you should say and there are things you should not say. A faith of positive statements. A faith where if you are sick you cannot say that you are sick because then you have no faith. A faith that if you are dying with pain you have to say "Healed by the wounds of Christ"

A faith that if you are starving you should say "Blessed and prospered" because this faith is based on declaring the opposite, because words have power. This modern faith says that if you are sick and you say you are sick, then it is a lack of faith and you open a door to illness.

This modern faith teaches that if you go to the doctor and, for example, he tells you that you have diabetes, your response should be "I reject all illness, I do not have diabetes, I am healthy by the grace of Christ."

I know closely of a case where a person went to the doctor and the doctor gave her a diagnosis and she rejected it and proclaimed the opposite and declared herself healthy and did not go to the doctor again because she had faith, and when her family finally told her They convinced me to go to the doctor, it was too late. It's sad right? But that is not biblical, Paul did not tell Timothy to declare himself healthy, rather he recommended a medicine that was used for his illness and we cannot deny for a moment that the Apostle Paul was a man of faith, it would be folly to question the faith of the apostle Paul, what we must begin to question is our perception of what faith is.

Something I have learned in this time is that, if I think something is one way, but it was not taught or practiced by Jesus or the apostles, then it means that I misunderstood that principle. And in the Bible people were never seen using these forms of faith that are used now, so surely, they should be discarded.

This gospel taught people to be hypocrites, if you feel sad you cannot say that you feel sad because a heart that has Christ cannot be sad. If you feel tired you cannot say that you feel tired because he will increase your strength. Like those of the buffalo, if you are sick, you cannot say that you are sick because you are healed by the wounds of Christ and if you say how, you really feel in front of other Christians, they crucify you for "your lack of faith."

We live before a generation of hypocritical Christians who do not tell the truth, but rather say what they must religiously respond to.

I remember a young woman with obvious signs of sadness on her face, I asked her how she was and she told me "Blessed and in Victory" my response was "Don't come to me with that stupidity of that modern fantasy faith, to me you tell me how you really "You feel and what is happening to you" at that moment the young woman was sincere and I was able to help her.

But this faith of this modern gospel not only makes people hypocrites but also slaves, you cannot imagine the freedom one feels when one no longer has to pretend, when one can be sincere.

Another problem of this modern faith that makes it a serious danger is that in many churches it is even taught to sign checks without having anything in the bank "by faith" because God does not leave his children ashamed. This new gospel has taught people to be deceivers, liars and irresponsible with the excuse of faith. They get into debts that they shouldn't get into; they commit to things that they shouldn't commit to because if you have faith God is going to work. Therefore, this faith has caused us to tarnish the name of the gospel.

But the truth is that none of that is faith. Even Jesus felt sad and expressed it. We never see the use of the positive statement in the Bible, he who was sick said that he was sick, he who was sad said that he was sad. The positive statement is not part of the Bible.

Does all this mean that we are going to walk around all the time like Mrs. Wailing or with the Ugly Duckling syndrome? Of course not. The apostle Paul was one of the most suffering apostles, however, he published a letter recognized as the book of joy, where he again and again urges the brothers to be joyful, this book is the letter of Philippians where we know that Paul was going through a moment of sadness because he expresses it clearly, without hiding it and without positivist statements in Philippians 2:27 but, despite that, we read verses like the following:

Philippians 1:18 What does it matter? At the end of the day, and no matter what, with false motives or with sincerity, Christ is preached. That's why I'm glad; What's more, I will continue to rejoice

Philippians 2:2 fill me with joy having the same mind, the same love, united in soul and thought.

Philippians 2:18 So you too, rejoice and share your joy with me.

Philippians 2:29 Receive him in the Lord with all joy and honor those who are like him,

Philippians 3:1 Finally, my brothers, rejoice in the Lord. It doesn't bother me to write the same thing again, and it gives you security.

Philippians 4:4 Rejoice in the Lord always. I insist: Rejoice!

I think my discovery in this area is already clear, but I'll summarize it like this:

"Faith does not deny reality, if I am sick, I accept that I am sick, and by accepting it is not that I am opening doors for the devil so that the illness can enter, because it is already there, but I pray with faith believing that he can heal me. Faith does not imply positive statements, Jesus did not say "I am blessed and in victory", but rather this happened "Matthew 26:38: Then Jesus said to them, my soul is very sad, even to death; stay here, and watch with me."

And in the Bible, we do not find those positive statements anywhere. "I accept reality, but I have faith in a God who can change that reality."

CHAPTER VI

Discovering The Biblical Truth about the Invariability of God.

The current gospel has wanted to show us a God who, since the New Testament, had a change of character. That in the Old Testament he was serious, jealous, but since the New Testament he became permissive, he accepts everything because since the death and resurrection of his son he is now pure love and has already left the consuming fire. A God who can be given orders, and told "I don't take no for an answer." A God who is forced to do whatever we want if we remind him of what he once said.

For this new gospel, the God of the New Testament is quite cool, he is not concerned with holiness and accepts us as we are, he does not judge us, he does not command us to repent like that God of the Old Testament who spent his time sending prophets with the lice. from "Repent, Repent"

This God of this new gospel rather sends prophets to say "You are going to be a millionaire" "Money is coming, Money is coming" "Your company is going to prosper" "You are going to have a new car" It is not to be doubted because this New God has enchanted today's materialistic society so much.

But I have news that will be very good or very bad depending on which side of the line you are on. The God of the Old Testament did not become an idiot after the resurrection of Jesus and now he endures everything and accepts everything because HE is pure love. Ask Ananias and Sapphira who he killed for lying to him (Acts 5:1-10)

The first prophet of the New Testament, John the Baptist, came with the same message as the prophets of the Old Testament: Repent! Let me tell you something that perhaps you do not know or perhaps you are not even interested in knowing: "What happens is that the majority of those who call themselves prophets today are not even prophets" but why do I say it? No! They simply do not meet the characteristics that the prophets of the Bible had.

Today's prophets do not speak of repentance, they do not correct, they do not warn, they only say nice things and no biblical prophet has those characteristics.

One of those current prophets once said: "I am not here to give bad news like those prophets of disaster, because God sent me like Isaiah to preach good news to the brokenhearted, (A) to bind up the brokenhearted, to publish freedom for the captives, and the opening of the prison for the prisoners" (Isaiah 61:1)

Obviously, the entire church was shouting "AMEN" euphorically. I think it was precisely after that that I decided to investigate what a prophet was. I started with Isaiah himself, and I said to myself, "That's chapter 61, let's see what's further behind." And what I found further back was not so nice.

I don't want to focus on this alone because I hope to write a book dedicated just to this topic of the prophets, but let's look at Isaiah chapter 1:

Isaías 1:2 Oíd, cielos, y escucha tú, tierra; porque habla Jehová: Crie hijos, y los engrandecí, y ellos se rebelaron contra mí. **Isaías** 1:3 El buey conoce a su dueño, y el asno el pesebre de su señor; Israel no entiende, mi pueblo no tiene conocimiento. **Isaías** 1:4 ¡Oh gente pecadora, pueblo cargado de maldad, generación de malignos, hijos depravados! Dejaron a Jehová, provocaron a ira al Santo de Israel, se volvieron atrás.

This pastor said that he was like Isaiah, that he had not been sent to give bad news, but apparently this pastor had not read the book of Isaiah very well.

I think I will never forget a prophet who in the middle of a service said, how many want me to prophesy to them? I will never forget it because it was another of the reasons why I decided to investigate the topic of prophets because I remember that at that moment, I said to myself "Is prophesying that cool?" But my Bible says that prophecy was never brought about by human will (2 Peter 1:21)

But don't get lost, Sunday, we're talking about it, it's from the New Testament, well the first prophet who appears in the New Testament said things like: When he saw that many of the Pharisees and Sadducees came to his baptism, he said to them: Generation! of vipers! (E) Who taught you to flee from the wrath to come? (Matthew 3:7)

And God himself incarnate said words like these:

Generation of vipers! (M) How can you speak good, being evil? Because of the abundance of the heart the mouth speaks. (N) (Matthew 12:34)

God has not changed, he is still the same God of love and fire, jealous and loving, sweet, but at the same time rigid. The same one who said to the woman "Neither do I condemn you" (John 8:11) But he said to scribes and Pharisees "Hypocrites and blind guides" (Matthew 23)

In short, no, God does not change, God did not become an idiot from the New Testament and continues to command us to fear Him **(Matthew 10:28)**

CHAPTER VII

Discovering The Biblical Truth about The Message.

Never in life has a gospel been preached so light, sweet, cool and easy as in our time. John MacArthur says: "The gospel has become so easy that I fear it is no longer the gospel."

Writing this I remembered how the way I expounded the gospel changed over the years depending on the church where I was, in the 80s in the Pentecostal church, Salvation, then in the free church my preaching was the wonderful group of young people we had and cool that the church was, then my preaching was to talk that we belonged to the largest ministry in the country, while I was on this journey of discovery I discovered that I was not the only ridiculous one to preach this way.

Today, the message of the gospel has become something as cool and easy as "God loves you and has a wonderful plan for you." The truth is, nowhere in the Bible was the message preached in this way.

The message of the gospel was totally changed to make it more pleasant, to not be offensive, to not hurt people's feelings. Above all, from this "Crystal" generation

I saw expositions of the gospel in the groups known as "Houses of Peace" that I was amazed because I had never in my life seen sin so downplayed or spoken so softly about repentance as in those places. In modern Christianity people are not made to see that they are sinners and therefore repentance is not seen as something very important.

But the message of the gospel is "REPENT AND CONVERT" (Matthew 3:2, Matthew 4:17, Mark 1:15, Acts 2:38, Acts 3:19) No, and NEVER IN HISTORY HAS IT BEEN: "God loves and has a wonderful plan for you." The problem is that churches have become companies where the goal is to fill places and to fill those places you have to attract people with a nice message and "Repent and convert" is not a nice message that attracts people.

Someone once told me, referring to the preaching of the gospel, "You can't marry flies with salt." It makes me think that the message of the gospel was not changed because of ignorance, but because of a change of purpose.

This week, someone's post on Facebook made me laugh, celebrating 18 years of ministry, and while I was looking at the photo of their celebration, I remembered an activity of theirs to which they invited me. The activity was intended to attract young people. And do you know what it was about? activity? Well, it was something quite spiritual, a swimming pool with the little sisters in bikinis! I saw the publication and I laughed to myself and told myself: "This is how they are going to reach 100 years of ministry."

I no longer remember the last time I heard preaching about the narrow gate, about the narrow path (**Matthew 7:13,14**), about denying yourself, about taking up the cross, about how you have to leave everything, even sacrifice love. of your family (Matthew 10:37,37) It is not preached that the gospel brings division (Luke 12:52) but it is preached that everything will be harmony, however, that is a lie, that is not the true gospel. The message was changed because it doesn't help with marketing.

World leaders of Christianity do not even like to talk about hell because it is offensive. But the root of the gospel is offense because the natural man does not like to be told that he is a sinner, which is why he feels offended and it is for this same reason that, as men of God such as John MacArthur, Paul have already explained time and time again, Washer, Miguel Núñez, Sugel Michelen, among many others; It is impossible to pretend to preach the true gospel without offense.

In short, the true message of the gospel is repent and convert, the message is that following Christ has a high cost and is a life of denying self and taking up the cross, but the entire message was deliberately changed for "marketing" reasons.", that is, to attract more people and it is more than clear that if people are "converted" with the wrong message it is impossible for them to really be converted.

CHAPTER VIII
Discovering The Biblical Truth About Cost.

I think this was one of the discoveries that caused me the most pain and with which I felt most betrayed by the current church, especially when I realized that I had never heard Hebrews 11:36-38 preached. Wonders were always preached up to verse 35 but they never talked about the following verses.

I firmly believed, just as the modern church teaches, that Christians do not suffer and if they suffer it is because they are not in the will of God. I was sure of all that until I read such verses from Hebrews that the modern church does not talk about. I also started reading books like "The Life of Trust" by George Müller and books about modern martyrs. Yes, believe it or not, I did not know that there were "those people" who suffered for the sake of the gospel. The last book I read on that topic was "Tortured for Christ" by Richard Wurmbrand and to be honest I still can't get over it.

The current gospel is always presented saying that God wants to bless you, in fact, I have seen calls where people were told "How many do you want to be blessed?" And of course, who is not going to repeat any prayer if it is to receive a blessing?

I have heard people tell that God is going to bring harmony in the family, they say that the husband who left the house is going to return, that the children who left are going to return. They tell them that they are going to have a life of happiness and joy.

FAKE! Perhaps a husband will return and perhaps a child will return, but the true gospel says otherwise: Luke 14:25-33, Luke 12:51-53, Matthew 10:34-38

In the current gospel the price of following Christ in the correct way is never talked about, but Jesus never ignored this issue, Jesus always explained the cost of following him:

Luke 14:26 "If anyone comes to me and does not sacrifice love[b] for his father and mother, for his wife and children, for his brothers and sisters, and even for his own life, he cannot be my disciple.

Luke 14:28 » But, don't start without counting the cost.

Luke 14:33 So you cannot become my disciple without giving up everything you own.

Luke 12:51 Do you believe that I came to establish peace in this world? No! I didn't come for that. I came to cause division.

Luke 12:52 In a family of five, three will be against the other two.

Luke 12:53 The father and the son will quarrel, the mother and the daughter will do the same, and the mother-in-law and the daughter-in-law will be enemies.

Matthew 10:34 »Do not believe that I have come to establish peace in this world. I have not come to bring peace, but disputes and difficulties.

Matthew 10:35 I have come to turn the son against his father, the daughter against his mother, and the daughter-in-law against his mother-in-law.

Matthew 10:36 You will have your worst enemy in your own family.

Matthew 10:37 »If you prefer your father or your mother more than me, or if you prefer your sons or your daughters more than me, you do not deserve to be mine.

Matthew 10:38 And if you do not carry your cross [4] and follow me, you do not deserve to be mine.

Matthew 10:39 If you only worry about your own life, you will lose it. But if you are willing to give your life for my sake, I assure you that you will win it.

As I have said before, I believe that the omission of cost in the current gospel has more to do with marketing issues than ignorance, if we talk about cost the gospel does not seem so pleasant and the number of converts is reduced and that is not very nice when churches have the forms of a company.

CHAPTER IX
Discovering The Biblical Truth About Identity.

For some years now people have been teaching about the identity of the Christian and I honestly don't see that it is bad to teach about that. It is important that each Christian be clear about his or her identity; the problem is that the way in which this topic is being taught is good, but very distorted. Usually, what we are taught is nothing more than pride, haughtiness and arrogance with a disguise of Identity.

We have been led to believe that we are all children of God, that we are all seated with Christ in heavenly places, and that we are the big deal. In fact, we were made to believe that no one should or could do anything to us because we are children of God.

We have been taught our rights as children, that we are kings and priests, that as children we are sitting at the table.

Romans 8:17 And if children, then heirs; (A) heirs of God and joint heirs with Christ, if indeed we suffer with him, so that we may be glorified with him.

That verse has been preached more than the song ♪♫How I Pay You♪♫ has been played on a mother's birthday.

And if we see it with the naked eye, everything looks good, but no, it is not good, because this very necessary teaching has been focused in such a bad way that some believe that they can give orders to God. Others taught us that we could tell God that we don't take No for an answer.

I always say that it is as if someone picked us up from a garbage dump, bathed us, put us in new clothes and sat us down to eat at their table and then we started giving orders to the person who rescued us and trying to force them to comply with our every whim.

And really that is what the bad teaching of identity in the church has done, it has made Christians proud, haughty, arrogant, because since they are Children of God no one can tell them anything.

It happens today that many people are rightly corrected by a leader or a boss in their work, it draws their attention and they respond "NOT ME, I AM A SON OF GOD!"

First, we cannot even affirm that everyone who attends a church is a child of God because to be a child there are requirements:

Matthew 5:44,45: But I say to you: Love your enemies, bless those who curse you, do good to those who hate you, and pray for those who despitefully use you and persecute you; 45 that you may be children of your Father who is in heaven, who makes his sun rise on the evil and the good, and sends rain on the just and the unjust.

Matthew 5:9: Blessed are the peacemakers, for they will be called children of God.

Luke 6:35 Therefore love your enemies, and do good, and lend, expecting nothing from it; and it will be your great reward, and you will be children of the Most High; because he is kind to the ungrateful and the evil.

John 1:12 But to all who received him, to those who believed in his name, he gave the right to become children of God;

John 12:36 While you have the light, believe in the light, that you may be children of light.

Romans 8:14 For as many as are led by the Spirit of God, these are children of God.

Philippians 2:14,15: Do everything without murmuring or disputing, that you may be blameless and innocent, children of God without blemish in the midst of a crooked and perverse generation, among whom you shine as lights in the world;

Hebrews 12:7,8 If you endure discipline, God treats you as sons; because what son is he whom the father does not discipline? But if you are left without discipline, of which all have been participants, then you are bastards, and not sons.

1 John 3:10 In this the children of God are manifested, and the children of the devil: whoever does not do justice, and who does not love his brother, is not of God.

So, even if you spend the whole day singing ♪♫ I am no longer a slave to fear, I am a child of God ♪♫ Maybe you are not even a neighbor.

I remember a person from a church who spent her time singing at the top of her lungs "♪♫ I am no longer a slave to fear, I am a child of God ♪♫" but there was one detail, no one could draw her attention and no one could correct her. because "She was a daughter of God" and precisely her attitude was showing that she was not really a daughter, but a bastard (Hebrews 12:7,8)

Another thing that is taught based on Hebrews 1:13,14 and that has made many Christians quite arrogant is that angels are there to serve us. Almost nothing! We are so super that the angels are there to serve us, but that is not what that passage really says. I like how it says it in the TLA version: "Because angels are only spirits that serve God, and he sends them to help all the people that God will save."

As we see, he does not say in any way that they serve us and that we can use them as servants as some who even give orders to the angels try to teach.

On the other hand, Jesus assured that his children who were like HIM would be mistreated, hated and even killed for the sake of Christ. Paul said that we would be or are the scum of the world. NO SPECIAL TREATMENT! If you are a true child the world will hate you, if the world loves you it means you belong to the world (John 15:18)

In short, it is good to know who we are, it is not bad to teach about the identity of the Christian, but the problem with this modern Christianity is that it distorts everything. G.K. said Chesterton "Falsehood is never so false as when it is almost true"

We are children if we meet the requirements, and we are children by grace. Someone described this truth in a song like this:

♪♫He is not like me, even though he has become a man and I call him by his name

He is not like me, although he has become flesh and my brother's name is

He is not like me, he transcends what exists and dresses in majesty.

There is no comparison ♪♫

Excerpt from the song "It's not like me" – Jesús Adrián Romero

Even though we are children of God, our attitude towards God and towards Jesus must be one of humility, gratitude and humiliation, because it was not by merit but by grace. We were rescued, bought, washed and sat at the table without deserving any of it. Therefore, as I said before, it is crazy to have an attitude of superiority or haughtiness or arrogance disguised as identity.

CHAPTER X

Discovering The Biblical Truth about Praise in the Church.

God had already been teaching me this part a few years ago, only at this time he confirmed many more things to me through his word.

Regarding music in the church, there are as many ideas of the way worship should be in the church, as there are stars in the sky, even though the book of psalms and the biblical references to the way worship is in heaven and also in the New Testament they give us clear directions of how our praise and worship of God should be, however, depending on the denomination, each person handles the matter of praise in different ways.

I practically grew up singing to the Lord, since I was a child in church I sang to God, all my life I have been surrounded by worship directors, praise leaders, singers, worshipers; and I have had to clearly know the difference between these last two, I have met those who are professionals and those who without much professionalism manage to touch the heart of God.

In my first years I grew up in an environment where God was given whatever and whatever because what God looks at is the heart, brothers sang songs to the Lord and the music went on one side, the one who sang on the other, and everything It sounded like horrible noises accompanied by screams, but everyone gave glory to God because what mattered was the heart. An environment where rehearsing mattered little because what does it is the holy spirit, they said. Rehearsing was considered to be like restricting the holy spirit from working.

Some say that everything should be calm, others use all kinds of instruments and others practically make a mess.

There were always several doubts within me, respect for all this, but the lack of biblical foundation prevented me from having firm convictions regarding the things I agreed with and those I didn't agree with. When I began this discovery, one of the verses that began to shape my convictions was Psalm 33 verse 3, the phrase DO IT WELL completely destroyed what I had been taught that God could be praised in any way. because what he looks at is the heart.

Little by little I began to understand that if your heart is correct you will seek to give it the best, that the fact of saying that God looks at the heart brings even more problems because when God looks at the heart, he will realize that it is not right. trying to give him the best, which is what he deserves. By that time, upon hearing the phrase "What matters is the heart" I understood that the person did not appreciate God enough to give him the best.

Of course, I am clear that there is the other extreme that I talked a little about in my book "Skeletons in the Closet" where I explain how people are so professional that their praise and worship of God lacks one of the main ingredients of worship of God which are sincerity and a broken heart.

These people use emotional manipulation, as I explained in my previous book, where a professional church singer told me that he didn't have to pray much to lead a service, that he just had to say the right words at the right time and he could make people cry in the middle of worship.

Unfortunately, there are plenty of these today and they even give workshops and conduct praise conferences of this type. People who have memorized the contents of the books of prominent worshipers and repeat them, but they do not have a life of seeking and a life of true prayer and worship.

I have seen with great pain how today people who only know how to manipulate emotions are recognized as great "anointed" worshipers. And it hurts a lot because what this shows is how the church is that does not know how to differentiate between what is Spiritual and what is emotional manipulation.

I firmly believe that the main characteristic of a worshiper is a broken heart (Psalms 51:17) but unfortunately, we live in a time where many people discovered that the spiritual can be imitated in the flesh and most do not realize it because there is no discernment. They make their faces, make the gestures, say the right words and make people cry, and that's it! They already have them as great worshipers. Not in vain does the Bible say that God is seeking those who worship in Spirit and Truth (John 4:23)

Now, this type of Christian singers manipulating emotions brought a problem, the problem is that because of them there are people who think that manifesting emotions and feelings while worshiping God is emotionalism, and any manifestation of emotions in the worship of God is already They want to call Kundalini and they call everything Strange Fire (Leviticus 10:1,2).

I remember reading a book, of which by the way I am not going to give even the name of the book or the name of the author, and I was surprised that for him every manifestation of emotions in the cult was "Strange Fire" and I said to myself, But What happens?! Simple, they went to the other extreme.

I had the opportunity to witness services of this type of people and the services look like funerals and that is not the biblical way either, God created us with emotions. And yes, the apostle Paul said that everything must be done in order (1 Corinthians 14:20) but he did not at any time say that emotions should be suppressed.

I, as I decided since I began this discovery, will focus on what the Bible says, my guide will be what the Bible teaches, what praise should be like in heaven and I will add a little of what John Wesley taught about praise. congregational.

King David and the book of Psalms in general teaches to praise God with a lot of noise, with a lot of joy and with every possible instrument, but doing it well and in order:

Psalms 51:17 The sacrifices of God are the broken spirit; You will not despise a contrite and humiliated heart, O God.

Psalms 33:3: Sing a new song to him: do it well, ringing for joy.

Psalms 32:11: You people of God, praise him and celebrate! And you, who are sincere in heart, sing to God with joy!

Psalms 47:1: Clap your hands happily, people of the world! Praise God with joy!

Psalms 63:5 I will praise you with my lips and shout for joy! That will satisfy me more than the most delicious food!

Psalms 81.1: Let out shouts of praise to God! He is our strength! Sing full of joy to the God of Israel!

Psalms 95:1: Let us sing to God with joy Come on, let us sing with joy!

Psalms 100:1,2: Sing joyfully to God, inhabitants of the whole earth. Serve Jehovah with joy; Come into his presence with rejoicing.

Psalms 107:22 Let us give him tokens of gratitude, and let us present offerings to him! Let us announce with shouts of joy the wonders that he has done!

Psalms 150:3-5: Praise him with the sound of a trumpet; Praise him with psaltery and harp. Praise him with tambourine and dance; Praise him with strings and flutes. praise him with resounding cymbals; Praise him with cymbals of joy.

1 Samuel 4:5: And it came to pass, when the ark of the covenant of the LORD came into the camp, that all Israel shouted with such great joy that the earth trembled.

Isaiah 6:1-3: I, Isaiah, saw God sitting on a very high throne, and the temple was covered under his cloak. This happened to me in the year that King Oziah died. I also saw some seraphim flying above God. Each one had six wings: with two wings they flew, with two others they covered their faces, and with the other two they covered themselves from the waist down. With a loud voice they said to each other: "Holy, holy, holy is the only God of Israel, the God of the universe; The whole earth is full of his power! »

Revelation 19:1,5,6: 1 After this I heard a loud voice from a great multitude in heaven, saying, Hallelujah! Salvation and honor and glory and power belong to the Lord our God; 5 And a voice came from the throne saying: Praise our God, all his servants and those who fear him, both small and great. And I heard like the voice of a great multitude, like the roar of many waters, and like the voice of great thunder, saying, Hallelujah, for the Lord our God Almighty reigns!

According to the Bible, true praise is very loud, but I have a Bible that also tells me that everything must be done in order, so I can be right by saying that I am neither bald nor have too much hair. In practice, I have seen how what I see in the book of psalms can be fulfilled, it can be praised with a thousand instruments, with shouts of joy, but at the same time with order.

I remember one time being in the praise group in my city that the pastor appointed a new praise leader and wanted to establish that everything was played and sung Jazz style, I said to myself, What? And those of us who didn't like the idea were called noisy and I told the pastors "But I don't believe that the biblical way is like that." Unfortunately at that time I didn't have as many arguments as I have now, in the end the pastor accepted what that worship leader wanted to establish.

I want us to be able to understand something, Christians do not do the things we like and we do not do the things we do not like. Christians must do things the biblical way, whether we like it or not. This is how it should be, the Bible should be above everything, but unfortunately this is almost never fulfilled because we put our tastes and desires before what the Bible says.

Many mistakes have been made in worship, for some worship directors they see it as a platform to show their talent, others as if it were a concert, some Christians, even pastors, have the praise time as a "while the preaching arrives" because preaching is what really matters because it is the word of God. Another half-truth as the modern gospel has accustomed us to.

In the contemporary history of the church, much importance was given to the topic of praise in the church, it was so important in the church that one of the most important ministries of antiquity, (that of the Wesley brothers) one of the requirements for appointing someone a pastor is that he should know about praise, but today one hears pastors preach and correct everything about praise! That one would like to tell them, "Hey Brother, start studying the Bible first and then talk, you're talking a lot of nonsense."

For King David, praising God was something serious and delicate, not everyone sang or played. Today they don't have a week of converts and they already have them, they don't even pray for 5 minutes and they already have them as musicians. Once as a worship director I opposed something like that and the pastor was going to kill me.

Before finishing with this chapter, I would like to recommend that you once again read my book "Skeletons in the Closet" and forgive me if I sound repetitive and perhaps you will think that I only want you to buy that book, but the truth is there where I explain several things about praise that I consider very relevant.

I want to conclude this chapter by sharing some material from the Wesley brothers that I love. It is about the direction of singing in the church taken from the Works of Wesley Volume IX pages. 229 and 230. I hope you find it useful:

Directions for Congregational Singing

To make this part of worship more acceptable to God and of greater benefit to you and others, be careful to observe the following instructions:

1. Everyone sing. Try to meet with the congregation as frequently as possible. Don't let a little weakness or tiredness stop you. If such a thing is a cross to you, take it up, and you will find it to be a blessing.

2. Sing loudly and vigorously. Don't sing as if you were half dead or half asleep. Raise your voice loudly. Be no more afraid to hear your voice, nor more ashamed to be heard now, than when you sang the songs of Satan.

3. Sing modestly. Do not shout, as if you want to stand out or distinguish yourself from the rest of the congregation, so as not to destroy the harmony. Everyone should try to join their voices with those of the rest of the congregation to produce a clear and melodious sound.

4. Sing on time. Whatever the time in which it is sung, try to keep it, do not get ahead or behind; Follow the guiding voices and go with their time as much as possible. Don't sing too slowly. Dragging time is a natural thing for lazy people and it is time for that habit to disappear from among us and for us to sing all our hymns just as we sang them at the beginning.

5. Above all, sing spiritually. Think of God in every word you sing. May your intention be to please him before yourself or any other creature. To achieve this, pay close attention to the meaning of what you sing and take care that your heart does not become too involved with the melody, but offer it to God continually, so that your singing may be such that the Lord can approve it here.

Although perhaps even the Methodists have forgotten this gem of teaching, that does not mean we should forget it too.

ANNEXES

55

What's wrong with the "prosperity gospel"?

God has made many promises and cares about our well-being. But does this mean that true Christians will always have health and wealth in this life?

Several years ago I had an interesting conversation with a believer in God in New Zealand. He firmly believed that if he asked God to heal him, God would always heal him. In fact, he believed that God had to heal him, without exception. I reminded him that we all die of something, whether due to illness, accident or old age, but nothing seemed to convince him.

I later realized that his thinking was very similar to a movement in Christianity known as the "prosperity gospel," the health and wealth gospel, or "ask and receive." Millions of Christians around the world profess some form of this modern gospel, and even some of the largest churches in the United States are at the forefront of the movement.

But what is the "prosperity gospel"?

In a New York Times op-ed, Kate Bowler, a historian of the prosperity gospel, said:

"Simply put, the prosperity gospel is the belief that God gives health and wealth to those who have the right faith... I discovered that the prosperity gospel in part emerged from the American metaphysical current of New Thought, an ideology of late 19th century according to which positive thoughts produce positive circumstances, and negative thoughts produce negative circumstances."

Bowler also explained that "variations of this belief were fundamental to the development of self-help psychology" (February 13, 2016).

A very attractive new gospel

Last year, a reader of our Life, Hope & Truth website asked, "What's wrong with the prosperity gospel?" This is a valid question.

Don't we all—whether we live comfortably or struggle with poverty, disease, or suffering—want to hear good news and have a good life now? Hearing that God wants to give us health and wealth at this time is certainly appealing.

Stephen Prothero, a renowned author and chair of the religion department at Boston University, explains: "Poor people like prosperity. Hears about her as a wannabe. Hey, 'You can do it too—buy a car, get a job, be rich.' It can function as a form of liberation" (quoted in "Does God Want You to Be Rich?", Time magazine, September 10, 2006).

Not surprisingly, a Time poll related to the previous article revealed that "17 percent of Christians surveyed said they consider themselves part of the movement, while 61 percent believe God wants people to be prosperous." In fact, "31 percent...believe that if you give your money to God, He will bless you with more money."

Time also explained that the focus of the prosperity gospel "is God's promise of generosity in this life and the ability of the saints to claim it. In short, it suggests that a God who loves us cannot want us to be broke."

As television evangelist Joyce Meyer said: "Who would want to get into something where they're going to be miserable and poor and ugly and just have to muddle through until they get to heaven?... I believe that God wants us to have good things" (quoted in Time).

Is the prosperity gospel true?

God does want to give us good, pleasant and spiritually rich things. But is the prosperity gospel in line with the message Jesus Christ preached when he came to Earth 2,000 years ago? Let us look at the words of Christ himself: "But seek first the kingdom of God and his righteousness, and all these things will be added to you" (Matthew 6:33).

What was first on Jesus' mind? The future Kingdom of God and the development of righteous character in preparation for that Kingdom. In the previous verses, Christ actually told his followers that they should not worry about food, drink, and clothing—the basic needs of physical life. God provides us with all that because he knows we need it. All other things in this life will also come if we put the spiritual first.

Shortly before, Jesus also said: "Do not lay up for yourselves treasures on earth... but lay up for yourselves treasures in heaven... For where your treasure is, there your heart will be also" (Matthew 6:19-21). God does not want us to fall into the trap of materialism. He wants us to learn to be giving as He is.

Again, Christ's focus was on God's spiritual treasures.

Jesus' message—his gospel—did not focus on health, wealth, or endless physical blessings for this life. Those who believe that his priority was physical blessings surely think that he failed to give those promised riches to the world.

What did Jesus Christ offer?

What Christ offered his followers was spiritual wealth, spiritual understanding. He explained to them the blessing of having a close spiritual relationship with God—being his children (1 John 3:1-3). He revealed the truth of why we were born: to become children of God and receive eternal life (Romans 8:14-17). And He desires that we all receive salvation in due time, along with the gift of eternal life in His Kingdom (1 Timothy 2:3-4).

Was Christ against physical blessings in this life? Certainly not. Some of his servants of old, such as Abraham, Solomon, and Job, were immensely rich and blessed with great abundance. However, it is also clear that others of his servants—known and unknown—went through great afflictions, poverty, and suffering. In fact, many of the saints died in terrible ways in martyrdom, but with their eyes fixed on the great future that God had promised them (Hebrews 11:13-16, 35-40).

The true gospel of God is not about

something physical that we can "ask and receive" now. We cannot force God to do our will. Instead, He calls us by His grace to know His way and the wonderful message of His future Kingdom, in which we will have eternal spiritual riches and blessings (John 6:44; Romans 14:17).

A Much More Subtle Prosperity Gospel: More Common THAN YOU THINK.

Although evangelicals have traditionally criticized the prosperity gospel in its "explicit" form, there is a more subtle form of this teaching that is very common among us [1]. Often undetected by Bible-believing Christians, it takes the gospel for granted and leads its adherents to focus on things like financial planning, diet and exercise, and strategies for personal growth.

In contrast to the "hardcore" prosperity gospel, which offers immediate, miraculous health and wealth, this softer variety challenges believers to move toward a life of blessing through the latest technique prescribed by the pastor. Of course, personal stewardship issues such as money, health, and leadership skills must be woven into a biblical theology of Christian discipleship. The problem arises when Christians, and especially pastors, place greater emphasis on these secondary issues. What we choose to preach or listen to says a lot about what we value. And what I see among some evangelicals is a willingness to prioritize the lesser matters of the law over the greater mercies of the gospel.

This is not a new concern. Others have described facets of this prosperity gospel under names such as moralistic and therapeutic deism, Christless Christianity, and the commodification of Christianity [2]. In truth, the three descriptions overlap to portray a prosperity gospel that could easily go unnoticed, because it seems reasonable to Christians who love God and the American dream.

A SOFTER AND SUBTLER GOSPEL OF PROSPERITY

It is obvious to those with eyes to see that such subtle signs of this form of prosperity are everywhere in Christianity. Christian radio offers a "positive and encouraging" experience with countless songs calling listeners to be "overcomers." Christian publishers market books that help Christians look better, feel more confident, and reach their full potential. Likewise, Jeremiah 29:11 and Philippians 4:13 continue to be erected as mantras by Christians who want to have an impact on the world.

But of course, these examples are just symptoms, and the solution is not to demonize Christian retailers. Rather, we must all learn to think more deeply about the content of our faith and refute the erroneous teachings of the subtle prosperity gospel (Titus 1:9).

FIVE MARKS OF VERY SUBTLE PROSPERITY

To aid in that discernment, let me outline five trademarks of very subtle prosperity, which appear particularly in sermons and books:

1. Subtle prosperity elevates "blessings" more than the blessed God

When blessings are divorced from the triune God, compromise occurs. True blessedness resides only in God, "the blessed and only Sovereign, King of kings and Lord of lords" (1 Timothy 6:15). Therefore, seeking God's blessing requires seeking Him (Isaiah 55:6-7, Matthew 6:33). Christ is the true treasure (Matthew 13:44-46), and any pursuit of blessing that makes God a means to an end is mistaken and idolatrous.

2. Subtle prosperity separates verses from the redemptive message of the Bible

When preachers present isolated verses as honest principles to claim God's blessings, they end up preaching a false gospel. Instead of relating all blessings to Christ, they directly apply isolated verses to people today.

Such a promise motivates the strong and quenches the weak. Unless a passage is correctly related to the Bible's redemptive framework, verses like Psalm 1:3 become treadmills on which fervent Christians exhaust themselves. Authentic Christ-centered expository preaching prevents this type of textual manipulation and guards against the soft prosperity gospel.

More specifically, subtle prosperity delights in the tangible promises of the Old Testament [3]. Error is often found in promising the blessings of the old covenant to new covenant saints. Every time we read the Old Testament, faithful interpreters must analyze; first, how the promises related to Israel in its historical and theocratic form; second, to Jesus who perfectly fulfilled the law (Matthew 5:17); and third, to us. Because we live under the new covenant, there will always be continuity and discontinuity between the Old Testament promise and its contemporary fulfillment. Preachers must learn to interpret these ancient texts at the textual, temporal, and canonical levels [4]. Likewise, healthy churches must learn to find every blessing in the relationship with Jesus Christ, the mediator of the new covenant.

3. Subtle prosperity diminishes the curse Christ endured and the blessing of the Holy Spirit

In the Bible, blessedness is not a vague idea. Deuteronomy 27-28 specifies the content of the blessings and curses of the Mosaic covenant. Citing these verses, subtle prosperity preachers teach that divine blessings come through greater obedience, but they ignore the fine print. Only one man has so perfectly obeyed God to merit God's blessing (Hebrews 10:5-10). And out of obedience, Jesus was condemned to death on a Roman cross, cursed for the sins of his people (Galatians 3:10-13).

Perhaps the biggest problem with subtle prosperity is the way it takes up the cross of Christ, instead of worshiping the Blessed One who bore the wrath of God in our place (Galatians 3:13), preachers of soft and subtle prosperity They often talk about what can be done to experience God's favor, but they rush past the cross, missing the fact that every spiritual gift has been secured for the believer through Jesus, who gives us his Spirit as the preeminent blessing. (Galatians 3:14, Ephesians 1:3). Although they do not deny the path of the Romans, they are driving on another road that goes in the same direction.

4. Subtle prosperity depends on the therapeutic techniques prescribed by the pastor

Taking the gospel for granted, subtle prosperity preachers fill the void with a plate full of therapeutic techniques; using the language of Zion, they emphasize the believer's good works. Despite not explicitly denying salvation by grace through faith, pastors who repeatedly insist on life tips, techniques, and strategies for saintly success undermine the faith once and for all delivered to the saints.

5. Subtle prosperity is largely aimed at first world, middle class problems

While the four marks above could be applied in many ways to "hard" prosperity preaching, there is still a significant difference. While "hard" prosperity preaching invites followers to name and claim, subtle prosperity preachers inspire the bottom-up motivation to achieve dreams. First, good health and wealth visibly demonstrate God's salvation; in the latter, preachers proclaim a religion of therapeutic solutions. To quote just one of his teachers: «Do I believe in the supernatural return at the moment of giving? Yes sir! Do I believe God blesses tithes and offerings? Yes I believe it. But why should we teach you how to claim a car without teaching you about car payments and loan interest rates?

Simply put, TD Jakes' message promises the same gold through a different line of credit: super-abundant faith mixed with well-ordered works. Simply put, this more subtle prosperity preaching appeals to first world, middle class people who are too busy living to examine a message that reaffirms their natural aspirations for success. Tragically, "believers" who buy into this false gospel will remain ignorant of their greatest need—atonement for sin before a holy God—unless they confront the true gospel of Jesus Christ.

A BETTER THEOLOGY OF BLESSING

In the end, the tragedy of the subtle prosperity gospel is the way it focuses on earthly improvements. By offering Christians their best life now, the eternal realities of heaven and hell are lost. This brings up the very real possibility that many who hear the subtle prosperity gospel are and will remain lost.

In response, Christians must learn to recognize the error of subtle prosperity. And we, especially pastors, must—prayerfully—work to free others from it. We must first confess the ways in which desires for earthly success have clung to our own hearts. Second, we must present the biblical gospel, which vastly exceeds the offering of holy success. We must exalt the riches of the true gospel and trust that when God's sheep hear his call to repent of their sin and cling to Christ, they will also sell their soft prosperity and receive as a gift the only treasure that counts: Jesus Christ, the only blessed king. .

[1] On the difference between the hard and soft prosperity gospels, see Kate Bowler's insightful study, Blessed: A History of the American Prosperity Gospel. New York: Oxford University Press, 2013), 78.

[2] In this order, Christian Smith with Melinda Lundquist Denton, Soul Searching: The Religious and Spiritual Lives of American Teenagers (New York: Oxford University Press, 2006); Michael Horton, Christian Christianity: The Alternative Gospel of the American Church (Grand Rapids: Baker, 2008), esp. 65-100; Stephen J. Nichols, Jesus Made in America: A Cultural History from the Puritans to the Passion of the Christ. (Downers Grove, IL: IVP Academic, 2008), esp. 173-97.

[3] See a list of such verses in Michael Schäfer's article, The Prosperity Gospel and Biblical Theology.

[4] For a helpful treatment of this approach, see Edmund Clowney, Preaching and Biblical Theology. (Phillipsburg, NJ: P & R, 1979).

Why Am I Against The Prosperity Gospel?

october, 27 2014 by Josué Barrios[1]

Theologian John Wesley once said:

"When I have money, I try to get rid of it as soon as possible so it doesn't find its way into my heart."

Let's be honest: That's something you'll never hear a prosperity gospel pastor say. What is that gospel? It is one that presents Jesus as a magical genie who wants to give us a life full of luxury and success here on earth. Nothing is further from reality.

"A false gospel cannot save anyone, but the true gospel is the power of God."

I hate that gospel. I hate it because I love the true gospel and I love my neighbor. I hate it because God hates it too, just as he hates sin. A false gospel cannot save anyone, but the true gospel is the power of God (Romans 1:16).

It is necessary for Christians to judge fairly and denounce what is wrong, that is part of proclaiming the truth that can save. Jesus did it, the apostles did it, and if we are Christians, we will do it. That's why I write this post.

In the prosperity gospel there is no cross, there is no holiness, there is no sin, there is no true Christ, there is no salvation. Unfortunately, there are millions of people who believe in this false gospel and call themselves Christians. Shouldn't we be worried about that?

---

1.   https://josuebarrios.com/author/josuebarrios/

To embrace the prosperity gospel is to fail to truly recognize the grace of God and the value of Jesus above all else.

Reasons to be against the prosperity gospel.

I am against the prosperity gospel because it does not preach the true Jesus or the true purpose of God for our lives, by taking verses out of their context. He mutilates the Word of God and treats it as if it were garbage.

I am against the prosperity gospel because those who preach it are fools, hypocrites, thieves and harm the spread of the true gospel. Thanks to the prosperity gospel, many people have the opportunity to unfairly generalize and say that all Christian pastors are profit-seeking hypocrites. This is a "gospel" that encourages atheism! In fact, exponents of the prosperity gospel do more harm to the spread of the gospel than Richard Dawkins' criticisms.

I am against the prosperity gospel because it offers people dead in their crimes and sins (as the Bible points out) what they want and not what they need. In reality it offers little and cannot transform people's hearts, but immerses them in placebos.

I am against the prosperity gospel because it has deceived many people and bankrupted them, while usually only those who preach it prosper. Furthermore, as some people against this false gospel have pointed out, earthly prosperity is what Satan promises to those who worship him (Matthew 4:9).

I am against the prosperity gospel because it says that a poor person has no true joy, that their current state of poverty is just a process to sanctify them that will come to an end and evidence their complete redemption when they are rich, successful and healthy. We know that a person who believes this will not have his soul satisfied when he is richer, if he ever becomes richer. Only God can fill our lives.

I am against the prosperity gospel because it encourages a lot of laziness in the congregations where it is preached (since it invites people to work less), and in the same way it promotes comparisons that do not please God ("That brother is going through a difficult situation because you are not tithing or loving God.

I am against the prosperity gospel because, as John Piper says, if God's love for his children was measured by our health, wealth, and comfort in this life, then God hated the apostle Paul.

I am against the prosperity gospel because the Bible teaches...

"But godliness accompanied by contentment is great gain; because we have brought nothing into this world, and without a doubt we can take nothing out. So, having sustenance and shelter, let us be content with this. For those who want to get rich fall into temptation and a trap, and into many foolish and harmful lusts, which plunge men into destruction and perdition; because the root of all evil is the love of money, which, by coveting some, they strayed from the faith, and were pierced with many sorrows."

(1 Timothy 6:6:10, RV60)

And it also teaches...

"Let your habits be without greed, content with what you have now; for he said, I will not forsake you, nor forsake you; so that we can confidently say: The Lord is my helper; "I will not fear what man can do to me." (Hebrew 13:5-6, RV60)

"I am against the prosperity gospel because Jesus is worth more than everything"

I am against the prosperity gospel because Jesus is worth more than everything this world can give us and everything death can take from us. When we have Jesus, the things we don't have we don't need.

Jesus > Money and "success" in this world.

Jesus taught that it will be difficult for a rich man to enter the kingdom of heaven (Matthew 19:23). That's because the rich tend to think they're so satisfied here on earth that they don't see the need to believe the gospel, be saved from the wrath of God, and go to heaven. Jesus also said that we must guard against all covetousness because a man's life does not consist of the abundance of the goods he possesses (Luke 12:15).

The prosperity gospel throws those wise teachings in the trash and directs people's attention to what is material and fleeting. When a person worships Jesus primarily so that He will give him money and success, he is actually worshiping those things and is being idolatrous.

When God sometimes increases our income, it is so that we give more and love more. Not so that we may accumulate for ourselves and lay up treasures in this world (Matthew 6:19-20).

Christians are not called to live as rich in this world, since...

How can we tell the world that Jesus is more than enough to fill our inner thirst if we live as if money and goods are what can actually fill it?

How do we tell the world that Jesus is worth more than everything else, if we are stingy with our possessions and want to accompany high salaries with expensive lifestyles?

"The salt of the world is not the "Christians" who seek to live like the gold of the world."

The salt of the world is not the "Christians" who seek to live like the gold of the world. The salt of the world are true Christians, those people who seek their greatest joy in God for the Glory of Him.

In short, I am against the prosperity gospel because I am for the true gospel. And if he were not against every false gospel, then he would not really be for the truth.

«No one can serve two masters; for he or she will hate the one and love the other, or esteem the one and despise the other. "You cannot serve God and mammon" (Matthew 6:24)

The first word of the gospel is not "love."

It is not even "grace." The first word of the gospel is "repent." From Matthew to Revelation, repentance is an urgent and indispensable theme placed at the very forefront of the gospel message.

Richard Owen Roberts

If you are preaching the gospel the right way it will be a scandal.

If you try to diminish the scandal you are no longer preaching the gospel.

Paul Washer

Through the death of Jesus, God's offended justice was satisfied and his wrath appeased, if that is not in your gospel, **You Do Not Preach The Gospel**.

Paul Washer

Correct Theology says:

God **DOES NOT HAVE** to bless me.

God **DOES NOT HAVE** to heal me.

God **DOES NOT HAVE** to prosper me.

FINAL WORDS

Forgive me for any mistake in the translation, I don´t have money to pay a translator but as I think that the content of this book y very important as well as the content of my other two books that I have written till now I decided to translate it by myself. Although I keep thinking that my book "Skeletons in the closet: Memoirs of a Pastor's Son" is super necessary for every Christian in the world. But let's keep within this.

At the end of writing this book I am very concerned that because of my desire not to make the book long I have made the mistake of giving very few biblical quotations, but it must be understood that my idea is not to convince you, since that is the work of the Holy Spirit, only I give you biblical arguments that serve as a map so you can do your search.

My concern about not making this book long does not come from some external entity, but rather from myself, I particularly do not like long books, although I have had to read several very long ones, but since I don't like them, I don't want to give to you something that I myself would not like to read. I just wanted to make that clear.

The Bible should be the guide of every Christian and its voice should be worth more than that of any pastor, prophet or teacher, no matter how anointed. The problem is that the current church has been taught to idolize its pastors with the excuse that it is honor. This idolatry has caused many Christians to put what the "man of God" says above what the Bible says. And we have allowed each person to interpret the Bible in their own way when the rule is that the Bible interprets itself.

The other horrendous error or rather, heresy that I heard recently, is that "Revelations are above everything." That is to say, the Bible can say that we should not worship images, but if "a man of God" says that God revealed that if you can worship images then that revelation can invalidate what the Bible says because "Revelations are above everything"

We live in this time where within our own ranks the Bible is being downplayed.

In my journey discovering the true gospel, I read more Bible than anything else and the books I read, I filtered every word those books said with the Bible. God knows how much I love Pastor Paul Washer, although I have not had the honor of meeting him in person, but the books that I read by him, I read them with the book on one side and the Bible on the other, because I could love him very much, but my love for him is not going to make me take away the main place that the Bible has.

As I wrote at the beginning of these closing words, perhaps because of my desire not to make the book long, perhaps I avoided some important verse, but my beloved, you have your Bible, you must read it, you must study it and you must understand that the Bible is above everything even if you believe that your pastor is so spiritual that God has him added to his WhatsApp group.

Every pastor deserves honor, but that honor should not make us place his words above what the Bible says, because it is no longer honor, but idolatry.

Please forgive me if you find any grammatical or other errors, I have tried to do my best, but I know that even with my best effort you may find one or more errors.

On the next page I have placed a brief bibliography of some of the books that were a blessing to me. I hope they are as valuable to you as they were to me.

Kisses to all, I am the profebubba
epbaliasmartingarcia@gmail.com
gonzalezdomingo@gmail.com

My previous book can be a great blessing to you:

https://bookskeletonsinthecloset.blogspot.com

RECOMMENDED BIBLIOGRAPHY

- A Brief Explanation of the Gospel of Jesus Christ - Paul Washer 3.0

- There is no other Gospel - Charles Spurgeon

- Ten charges against the modern church - Paul Washer

- What is the church - R.C. Sproul

- Tortured by Christ - Richard Wurmbrand

- What has happened to worship - A. W. Tozer

- Why Revival Doesn't Come - Leonard Ravenhill

- Spurgeon's Sermon Collection

- A Simple Christianity -John MacArthur

- The One True God - Paul Washer

- Designed to Worship - A. W. Tozer

- The Gospel According to Jesus Christ - John MacArthur

- True and False Repentance - Charles Finney

- The Life of Trust - George Mueller

- The True Gospel of Christ versus The False Gospel - L. R. Shelton, Jr.

- Texts out of Context - Jairon Namnon

- A Simple Christianity - John MacArthur

- I Call It Heresy - A. W. Tozer

- Truth in War - John MacArthur

- The daily life of the first Christians - Fernando Rivas

- Skeletons in the Closet:
  https://bookskeletonsinthecloset.blogspot.com

- Diarios de Avivamientos:
  https://diariosdeavivamientos.wordpress.com/

Elprofebubba.blogspot.com

Also by Domingo Gonzalez

Una Gloria Diferente
A Different Kind of Glory
Un Tipo de Gloria Diferente - Domingo Gonzalez Jr.
Mi Travesía Descubriendo el Evangelio Verdadero - 2da Edición
Esqueletos no Armário - Memórias do Filho de um Pastor.- 2º. Edição.
Domingo González Jr.
Minha Jornada Descobrindo o Verdadeiro Evangelho.
My Journey Discovering The True Gospel - 2nd Edition - Domingo
González Jr.
Um Tipo Diferente de Glória - Domingo González Jr.